CHAMPION BY
CHOICE

Inspirational Publishing
rights@inspirationalpublishing.co

ISBN: 978-0-578-50716-3 (print)

Ordering Information:

Special discounts are available on quantity purchases by corporations, associations, and others. For details, contact rights@inspirationalpublishing.co

CHAMPION BY CHOICE

William Hung

For my parents, who always supported me,
even when I baffled them.

CONTENTS

Introduction 1

1: The World's Worst Singer? 5

2: My Beginning 15

3: The Dream Life 23

4: Discovering What You Want 31

5: Champion by Choice: Key 1
   Communicate and Speak the Truth 37

6: Your Stories Are Valuable 47

7: Leveraging Failures and Frustrations 51

8: Champion by Choice: Key 2
   Context 57

9: Changing Your Perception About Risk 65

10: Maximize Your Impact 75

11: Champion by Choice: Key 3
    Connect with the Right People 81

12: How to Add Value to Others 87

13: Treating People with Respect 93

Conclusion: Turning Your Dreams into Reality 97

Acknowledgements 101

INTRODUCTION

Everyone eventually hits rock bottom. Most people don't do it on national television, on the most popular show on TV, and in one of the most embarrassing ways possible. But that's how I did it.

If you're reading this book, you've probably seen it: My audition for *American Idol*. If you haven't seen it, it goes something like this: You would show up at a huge baseball stadium among thousands of other *American Idol* hopefuls, wait for hours for your name to be called, and then try to impress the *American Idol* staff members in 15-30 seconds. Yes, this is not what you see on TV, but it is the first step. Then if you make the cut, you get a chance to audition in front of the producers...and then the three celebrity judges: Randy Jackson, Paula Abdul, and Simon Cowell.

Typically, you can expect to get trashed by Simon Cowell. He is infamous for being the mean judge with his signature brutal honesty, and I was no exception. I was harshly criticized by him. I did not make it to Hollywood, and at the time, I thought I was nothing special.

Now you might be wondering: Why would you turn to me, of all people, for advice about success? Let me begin by assuring you that no matter how badly you may have failed at something, your failure probably wasn't as public as mine (or viewed on *YouTube* as many times). But here I am: A recording artist who is frequently asked to speak to large crowds and who has now written his first self-help book. So, trust me when I tell you that failure doesn't have to be a permanent condition.

As a matter of fact, failure is often a prerequisite to success. My message for you is not simply that you can succeed *despite* your failures but that you can succeed *because* of your failures.

In any endeavor, your opponents will seek out your vulnerabilities and try to exploit them. But what if you wear your vulnerability like a badge of honor? What if you use everything in your arsenal to your advantage—not only your strengths but also your weaknesses?

I have a certain advantage in that I've embarrassed myself in the most public way imaginable. It's over and done; I've faced my fear and moved on. I've stopped worrying about what my detractors think about me. I had to because the alternative was to stay stuck as a failing civil engineering student. I had to, because if I had stayed silent, I would have allowed everyone to speculate about my true identity and the real story behind my *American Idol* audition. Nowadays, I speak to audiences regularly in order to inspire people to go for their dreams by embracing failure, secure in the knowledge that no matter how awful the result might be, it's not going to be any worse than what I went through. Can you say the same? Do you feel that same confidence?

We're taught from an early age to fear failure. During my elementary school years in Hong Kong, although my parents did not pressure me to get rank 1 (the highest rank possible), I still felt the pressure because not getting into the top 3 ranks, rank 1 to rank 3, would mean that I wouldn't be able to go to a decent middle school and high school. I saw from Hong Kong TV dramas how getting into a bad middle school and high school could be a total disaster for the rest of one's life, like being coerced into joining the various gang groups.

This also matched what I saw on the news! I saw and understood why other parents would get extremely upset with their sons or daughters if they didn't get the higher ranks. There were 10 ranks possible and I was somewhere in the middle, between rank 4 and 6.

But I think that mindset is misguided. By embracing our failures, we disarm them of their power over us. And when the fear of failure is removed, there is no limit to what we're capable of.

I used to worry a lot about how I presented myself in public—like every word I said, what I wore, how I walked, and so many things that are not that important.

If you want to tap into the reservoir of potential that you have, you have to be willing to risk failure. I tried so many things in life and I failed with lots of them—not just singing but video game competitions, trivia competitions, and sales, including selling myself during job interviews.

Nothing great was ever accomplished without risk, and what most people I meet are worried about risking is their dignity. Don't get me wrong, dignity is a wonderful thing—but it can also be an impediment to development. It's easy to succeed at something you're naturally good at, but it's so much harder when you are naturally bad at it.

In the pages that follow, I intend to share my story of "getting back up on the horse." My hope is that you'll see your own life's journey reflected back to you, as my trajectory is only unusual insofar as it may involve a steeper ascent from its low point. We all fail, but those who succeed are those who use failure as a tool rather than as an obstacle.

With that in mind, let me take you back in time to a world in which America was not familiar with my name; a world in which my failures and successes were private. In other words, let me take you back to the time before that life-changing moment when I decided to become a contestant on the biggest talent show the country had ever seen.

CHAPTER 1

THE WORLD'S WORST SINGER?

I 'll never forget the day I heard the news. It was a day that would change my life, although I had no idea how at the time. I was watching the nightly news on FOX TV and they announced that *American Idol* would be holding an audition in San Francisco. I was attending college at Berkeley, so the venue was nearby.

Earlier that semester, I had experienced something similar, albeit on a much smaller scale. I discovered a flyer announcing a talent show at the Clark Kerr dormitories. I was really into Ricky Martin and I had recently been watching his live performance online of "She Bangs." It was my favorite song. I had been singing karaoke since I was 10 years old in Hong Kong, but I had never entered singing or talent competitions before, so I did not expect to win. Still, I felt like I had nothing to lose, so I said to myself, "Why not?"

I was the very last person to perform that night, and I didn't know how my friends and classmates would respond. But after I performed, they gave me a standing ovation with loud cheers. I didn't know if that was good enough to win, but it turned out that it was! I took home the grand prize: a brand new DVD player!

When I had decided to compete in that talent show, I wasn't sure how I would measure up. I did not feel that I was necessarily the most talented, but one of my main aims in life is to do what feels right in my heart. I thought to myself, "If I could win the talent show at school, why not take it to the next level?" My mom would often mention to me how she admired tennis pro Michael Chang and prolific figure skater Michelle Kwan, and then she would add that she'd like to hear my name, William Hung, mentioned on TV.

So, I thought the *American Idol* audition could be my golden opportunity. And the truth was that I was dreading having to go to class each day as a civil engineering student. Therefore, I felt it was better to try, even if it resulted in failure, than to live with the regret of not having made the attempt.

The more I thought about it, the easier it was to picture myself having the freedom to travel around the world to perform, making way more money than with civil engineering, and enjoying a much more exciting life. There was a sticking point, however: my parents.

As the son of elderly, conservative Chinese parents, my role was to buckle down and get good grades. They wanted me to be an engineer, a lawyer, a doctor—basically anything but an entertainer. Needless to say, they would be less than thrilled about me pursuing a singing career.

Fortunately, I came up with a brilliant solution that would make everyone happy: I just wouldn't tell them.

I told some of my close friends that I wasn't feeling well, and I remember asking one of my friends to take notes for me for one of the classes. I seriously did not expect to get past the preliminary rounds, but I knew I needed to give myself a chance to create a better life for myself.

I woke up really early on the day of the audition, as I felt like I had to rush if I was going to get in line by 7:00 a.m. It was one of those breezy San Francisco mornings, so I put on a jacket and jumped on the BART.

When I got to Pac Bell Park, 3,000 other aspiring singers were already arriving, and I could see that many people were taking the audition very seriously. There were very few people like me, who appeared to be there just for fun. So, I didn't want to expect too much because I knew the odds were against me, even if I had musical talent. One of the contestants had come all the way from Nashville, while another announced, "This audition is life or death for me."

I knew my odds of getting to Hollywood were slim. I thought

to myself, "If I make it to Hollywood, fantastic! If not, it will still be a valuable experience." I expected the *American Idol* judges to say something like, "No, that's not good enough. Sorry."

My plan was simply to do the same thing that had won me the talent show at college. Win or lose, it wouldn't be a big deal. Not because I didn't want to win. Rather, I wanted to focus on what I could control—performing my best with what I had. I planned to sing a different song this time. Instead of the Ricky Martin tune, I decided on "Two Worlds," by Phil Collins, so I could better showcase my vocal range.

Some people who showed up with friends discussed strategies to impress the producers and ways to hit certain notes. Most people were too busy rehearsing to even talk to me. So, while I waited in line, I rehearsed as well.

As I waited, I saw hundreds of people get a brief opportunity, and I do mean brief—about 15 to 30 seconds—to perform for the *American Idol* staff members before being told to go home.

And yet, surprisingly, they let me sing for over a minute and they let me through!

One of the female judges, Megan Michaels Wolflick, who asked me to come back for another audition—an event that would change my life—turned out to be an influential producer on the show, and she invited me to show up the following morning at the San Francisco Radisson Hotel for the next round.

I told her about my experience winning the talent show at the college, and she suggested that I go back to singing the Ricky Martin song rather than the Phil Collins song. She also told me that I should dress better for the upcoming audition.

That night, the FOX news program announced that of the 3,000 contenders, only about 180 had been selected to continue. I thought to myself, "Wow! Is this possible?" I had no reason to believe, at the time, that I had been chosen for any reason other than that I had been good enough to make the cut.

I rummaged through my closet for the right outfit, and I settled on a blue Hawaiian shirt. I thought it would help me stand out from the other contestants. I still did not want to tell anybody about my audition because I hadn't made it to Hollywood yet.

The next morning at the Radisson, I auditioned in front of a new group of producers. And, just like at the talent show, I performed "She Bangs." They seemed excited, and once again, they let me through.

At this point, there were only about 100 people left.

Then I found myself in front of the cameras, looking directly at Randy Jackson, Paula Abdul, and Simon Cowell. I had no idea what to expect. I knew from the outset that Paula was usually very nice and that Simon could be harsh.

As soon as I began to sing, Randy lifted a sheet of paper to his face to cover his laughter and he giggled throughout the audition. I knew then that I wouldn't make it to Hollywood. Still, I kept singing my best.

Paula seemed to enjoy my performance and watched politely.

Somewhere in the middle of the chorus, Simon stopped me. In his cockney accent, he said, "You can't sing, you can't dance, so what are you going to say?"

My disappointment was palpable as I thought about how to respond. I knew the judges were simply playing their roles. I wanted to keep things positive and not take anything personally. I remembered something my mom had told me, "It's okay to fail as long you tried your best."

I replied, "I already gave my best. I have no regrets at all."

"Good for you," Paula said, "That's the best attitude yet."

I explained that I didn't have any professional training, to which Simon replied, "Now this is the surprise of the century!"

I walked out of the audition room with my head held high. I had made a conscious choice to stay positive in a negative situation.

Although we don't have control over how other people treat

us, we do have a choice in how we respond. One of the contestants, I recall, had to be restrained by security and escorted out because he threw a water bottle at Simon. It never occurred to me to get sad or angry.

That guy who threw the water bottle received a lot of negative press but that may have been what he had in mind. My intention was simply to do my best and have fun. I wasn't out to do something weird just to get a little bit of fame out of the audition.

As far as I was concerned, it was over and it was time to get back to class. Nothing ventured, nothing gained. This was the end of the road in terms of my singing career, and my life would simply return to status quo. Or so I thought.

Then, suddenly, four months later, there was an ad that hit the airwaves during the FOX broadcast of the 2004 Cotton Bowl. And lo and behold, I was featured. I said to myself, "Oh no, what's happening? Why are they highlighting my audition?" But despite that glimpse, the reality of what would happen did not sink in.

Then later that month, my episode aired. I watched it alone in my dorm room. I hadn't been able to objectively evaluate my performance while I was in the middle of it. But now, removed from it and watching it on primetime, I saw what everyone had seen: A guy pumping his fists and twisting his hips like he was doing samba exercises. I had really exaggerated my body movements. Not my finest moment.

Still, I felt that I shouldn't be too hard on myself. The most important thing was that it had been fun. I had enjoyed the experience.

Immediately after the broadcast, my inbox began filling up with emails, *hundreds* of them. They were from people offering me performance opportunities and wanting to interview me.

Later that evening, local FOX news anchor John Beard announced, "William Hung is the worst singer ever." I didn't want to go out that night because I had no idea how my peers and classmates would react.

The next morning, I was afraid to go back to the classroom. I kept my head down and went to class, wanting to pretend that nothing unusual had happened.

At some point in the afternoon toward the end of one of my civil engineering classes, my professor decided to re-air my audition in front of the class—a class of hundreds of students. I thought to myself, "No! Why are you doing this?" My professor did not announce beforehand what he was going to do. I remember he said something about "a surprise from one of your classmates!"

After the class, as I tried to slip out, students mobbed me for pictures and autographs. I had fans! From that day forward,

I knew my life would never be normal again. I had achieved overnight celebrity. I talked to the professor and it turned out that he was one of my fans too!

My life's course had been inexorably altered. I was on the surreal path toward becoming an entertainer. And it's why I tell everyone that they must never give up on their dreams. My dream at the time was to become a professional entertainer.

My parents found out about my audition a few days later. In an awkward phone call with my mom, she said she had seen me on TV. "What happened?" she asked. "How come I didn't know about it?"

I explained that my dream was to become an entertainer. I told her that if I had never taken a chance at becoming an entertainer, I was eventually going to regret it. I also told her that I felt I couldn't tell her beforehand because I knew she would say no.

That rift with my parents lasted for a few months before they finally accepted that this was what I was going to do. Of course, my parents wanted me to go for a stable job with a stable income. But I realized I was going to be a professional entertainer who would bring joy and laughter to my audience.

And, to their credit, when I got the record deal from KOCH Records to put out singing albums, they became my manager and agent. As an only child, I was definitely overprotected, but I understood that it came from a good place.

CHAPTER 2

MY BEGINNING

My mother was born in what was then Burma, now known as Myanmar. Like many of the inhabitants, she was born into poverty, along with her five brothers and sisters. When she was still a child, the family moved to Macau. She and her family survived on a daily diet of two cans of meat or sardines, a duck egg, and rice, and she played with discarded dolls and bottle caps.

My father also grew up poor, in Macau. Macau is next to Hong Kong and Guangzhou in Mainland China. He was one of 11 children, and as a child, he worked on farms, picking vegetables and helping his mother sell them. He eventually went to vocational school and became a jewelry model maker, a far less lucrative profession than designing the jewelry, and he supplemented his income by driving a taxi.

It was in Hong Kong that he met my mother. She went there

after finishing school and got a job as a cashier. She also went there in search of a husband. Long story short, they got married and had a child (me).

I recall them bickering often as I grew up. He would sometimes lose his cool and blow up. Then, she would say he wasn't sensitive to her feelings and tell him that she only married him because they shared a traditional mindset. That's true for the most part. My mother was very conservative, and she wanted me to earn good grades, go to college, and get a respectable job. My father, meanwhile, took a more liberal approach, urging me to be realistic in my goals. There's a subtle but important difference because my dad was okay with me choosing a career and life that was not the norm. He just wanted me to figure out how I could thrive in whatever career I chose.

Divorce, for them, was never really an option, as in the Chinese tradition it is considered disgraceful to the entire family. The only way she would divorce her husband, my mother said, was if he were to lose all their money gambling, physically beat her, or cheat on her.

So, I witnessed their fights without the solace of a sibling's shoulder to lean on. Siblings can be confidantes in a way that parents simply can't, regardless of the strength of the relationship. Communicating my innermost feelings doesn't come naturally for me, and I've tended to rely on close, trusted friends when sharing my emotions.

One thing I always shared with my parents, however, was a passion for singing. When I was 10 and living in Hong Kong, they used to take me to lunch on weekends and we would sing karaoke. I loved The Four Heavenly Kings: Leon Lai, Jacky Cheung, Aaron Kwok, and Andy Lau. They were the most popular singers in Hong Kong at the time. But I was only comfortable singing Leon Lai, so I spent a lot of time learning his lyrics.

I also enjoyed playing video games. In fact, it was with video games that I first felt a competitive spark. Arcade games were all the rage back then and I'd wait my turn at the machine like everyone else. When my turn came around, I never wanted it to stop, and that desire drove me to improve my game. If I lost a life, I'd have to get back in line, so I got very good at staying alive. It was also a chance to impress my peers, of course, and in time, I was able to defeat the game in a single run without losing a single life.

Later that year, in 1993, we moved to America. My parents and I moved to Hershey, Pennsylvania because my dad got a job offer there. Unfortunately, my dad got laid off after just six short months, and we then moved to Los Angeles, California. My dad got a much better job there, and my parents were happier because they could connect with the Chinese community. They could go to Chinese cultural events, enjoy Chinese food, and listen to news from Hong Kong and mainland China. As for me, the biggest challenge was communicating fluently in English.

I remember I was in the fourth grade and hooked on Super Nintendo, and I felt the same competitive spark that I had back in Hong Kong. Soon after, I heard on the news that Blockbuster Video was holding a Donkey Kong Country tournament. That started my journey into competitive entertainment. I took sixth place locally, and I also learned that there were a lot of competitive video gamers out there. After the competition, I realized that I didn't have that same urge to be the best; I just wanted to have fun.

Simon Cowell's mean-spirited comments weren't the only experience I had with bullies. Prior to that, I had faced worse than a few unkind words. That's why I was able to take it in stride. Back in middle school, there was a kid who just didn't like me. I don't know why, but from the first day in class, he had it out for me.

I remember he would stare me down and then point at me and laugh. That's hard to cope with when you're someone trying to assimilate in a new country, and I felt that life was unfair. I kept thinking, "Why me? What did I do wrong to other people?" But it got worse. One day, he punched me in the arm. I hadn't done anything to deserve it, so I hit him back. Our melee drew the teacher's attention, and we stopped.

Of course, I didn't want to escalate the problem, so I ignored the kid, hoping that would be the end of it. But it wasn't. At lunch, he found me and punched me right in the eye, so hard that I felt dizzy. Out of my left eye, I saw him: My bully. I thought I would be blind in my right eye for the rest of my life. I couldn't open my eye for several hours, and I thought that my life could be over.

I explained what had happened to my parents, who complained to the principal. When he opted to suspend the boy for three days, my parents were livid, "What? You only gave him a three-day suspension?! What if my son had hit him back? Would *he* get a three-day suspension?" The principal told them that they could call the police if they didn't like it.

With that, my mother went to the LA Unified School District school board to plead her case to allow me to switch schools. And that's what I did. That wasn't the end of the bullying, but at least I never got sucker punched again. I remember that my graphic calculator was stolen and that I was pushed out of the food line and had to get one of the teachers to make things right. These events made it hard for me to trust any of my classmates. If I learned anything from the pain of those formative years, it was that not everyone you meet is going to like you and sometimes for no good reason. But you can't let it stop you.

It's hard enough being an only child but when you're an only child who gets bullied, you lack an enforcer or, at the very least, an ally. The incident scarred my childhood, and as a result, I put my trust not in my fellow students but in my teachers. Although I had a few friends, I felt I could be genuinely close only to adults like my parents and the teachers. I felt much more comfortable sharing my ambitions and my vision for the future with them.

My lasting memory from high school, much like my lasting memory of my burst onto the national stage, is bittersweet. I was in a math and science magnet program at Francis Polytechnic High School in Sun Valley. I was good at math but I had to work extra hard to be good at science compared to most of the students. To compensate, I gave up a lot of fun activities after school and on weekends in order to study. To make matters worse, the teacher was less than helpful. I relied on the AP exam book, a thick 500-page manual filled with chemistry minutiae, to figure things out.

Eventually, all of my hard work paid off when I was the only person in my class who passed the AP Chemistry exam. I earned college credit and never had to take chemistry again.

Afterward, I learned about a team competition called the Science Bowl. It was a trivia competition hosted by LA's Water and Power Department that covered the disciplines of math, chemistry, astronomy, physics, computer science, and earth sciences. My role was to focus on math, chemistry, and earth sciences—my strong subjects.

Our team did well by going 5-1 in the round-robin format

and earning us a spot in the semifinals. That meant we would be televised. And if you think I bombed on *American Idol*, you didn't see my performance at the Science Bowl. My brain shut down. For the life of me, I couldn't answer a single question correctly. During the preliminary rounds, I had been able to answer some of the questions from my strong subjects very quickly, within two to five seconds, once I knew what they were asking for. But in the final round, only my teammates were able to answer some of the questions correctly, so that made me feel like I was a dead weight for the entire team. It was absolutely humiliating, and (though I didn't know it at the time) a preview of things to come.

But, just like the experience with the bully, this embarrassing failure positioned me well for handling my next televised disaster. Being named on local TV as the "worst singer ever" by a news anchor might have stung more had I not already taken my licks and learned to cope.

The experience helped prepare me for future meltdowns, but it also gave me a more interesting way to do some extra studying. I put in more time and effort than I normally would have. The Donkey Kong Country competition that I had lost so many years earlier was suddenly paying dividends: the competitive drive it had sparked during my childhood would result in me earning valedictorian honors and, ultimately, an offer to attend UC Berkeley, among other universities.

That competitive nature I discovered while playing an arcade game ultimately got me into my college of choice. I may have lost the video game competition but my passionate striving resulted in greater rewards down the line.

So too, I may have lost the Science Bowl competition (and in face-planting fashion!) but I learned how to get back up after a humiliating knockdown, which altered the trajectory of my life.

CHAPTER 3

THE DREAM LIFE?

Naturally, I was excited when I first got into UC Berkeley. I had done well in school all my life, and although I knew college wouldn't be easy, I felt it was just one more challenge to overcome. I was wrong. Even classes like calculus and physics that I had previously done well in were like foreign languages. Linear algebra might as well have been taught in Martian.

With every passing day, I became more lost. Nevertheless, I somehow managed to pass those classes by getting enough of the easy questions right at exam time. I also did well enough with my humanities classes and electives, so I felt like I was doing enough to get by.

And then I got my first "D." It was in one of my civil engineering classes—my major, and I was put on academic probation. My spirits sank and I became depressed. I felt like I would never be able to live up to my parents' expectations of my becoming a successful civil engineer. Although I didn't care much about becoming a successful civil engineer, I didn't want to let my parents down after they had put in so much effort to get me where I was. The civil engineering program at UC Berkeley was the #1 program in the US at the time and one that would pave my way to a lucrative career, but it was not easy to get into.

To cope with my depression, I dove into a video game: Final Fantasy X, one of the most popular role-playing games at the time on PlayStation 2. I logged about 200 hours in that world while escaping this one.

I might have stayed there, too, had I not found an Asian Bible study group with other civil engineering students going through similar struggles. I told one of my classmates how I was depressed about studying for these classes, and he told me maybe I could join the Asian Bible study group on Friday nights to hang out, relax, and have fun. This actually helped me to turn things around. We collaborated on homework assignments and projects, and we studied for exams together. Then my grades finally improved. I wasn't getting As, but my Ds turned to Cs, and my Cs to Bs. And I was taken off academic probation.

Despite the improvement, something still felt very wrong; I dreaded getting up and going to class every day. I don't know what would have happened had I continued down that path.

But something changed my course: A flyer at the Clark Kerr dormitories advertising a school talent show. I remembered that I had started singing karaoke with my parents when I was 10 years old. To prepare, I started watching Ricky Martin music videos online, and one of the songs, "She Bangs," had a unique catchy tune I couldn't resist. I decided to give myself a chance. I had no expectations, but somehow I won the school talent show! This is what gave me the confidence to audition for *American Idol*.

After my appearance on *American Idol*, everything changed. I suddenly had fans on campus. I was interviewed by Ryan Seacrest and Ellen Degeneres on their respective shows. I was interviewed on *Entertainment Tonight*. Then, one of my fans built me a website, www.williamhung.net, which received more than eight million hits in less than a month!

Soon afterward, I was invited to perform once again at the Clark Kerr dormitories in front of a jam-packed room of several hundred students, and the emcee gave me a "Lifetime Achievement Award."

Next, I was invited to perform at a UC Berkeley men's volleyball game. By now, I figured it would be just another performance opportunity, but it wasn't. After the show, KOCH Records approached me to say they were interested in offering me a $25,000 contract.

My parents reviewed the contract with me and there were

some unfavorable terms, like traveling to promote my record album at least once a week. Traveling back and forth from the West Coast to the East Coast could definitely cause burnout. We considered rejecting the deal entirely, but one of KOCH's senior executives talked me out of it. He said we could work everything out and he asked me to think about it.

So, I prepared for one of the most important performances of my life. My friend, Betty Hsu, helped me to choreograph a dance routine, and she and some other friends worked hard rehearsing the number with me. She gave me suggestions on my own movements and advised me on how best to coordinate with the other dancers.

We put on a good performance, which was broadcast on TV. There were stations from all over the world that had shown up just for the event. Immediately afterward, someone from KOCH Records approached me and presented me with a $25,000 check for my record contract. They held a press conference for me and asked me whether I was ready to move forward with the record contract. I said I would need some time to think about it.

If I was going to commit to the record deal, I couldn't do it halfway. I would have to devote myself to my work as a professional entertainer and I wouldn't be able to do my college workload on the side. I quickly learned from other professional entertainers that most of the money would come from live performances. Besides, I was barely able to manage my school workload when it was the only thing on my plate.

Many people at the time considered the decision a no-brainer. After all, who would pass up a lucrative, once-in-a-lifetime opportunity? At the time, I was getting paid $10,000 to $20,000 for each live performance. Some of the commercial deals were worth over $25,000 each. It may not have been enough to retire on but what mediocre student who only recently got off academic probation would continue pursuing a career in civil engineering when he could instead become a pop star?

Others, however, viewed the opportunity as a distraction. Some fellow Asians even suggested that I was being used as a laughing stock, that they only wanted to perpetuate certain Asian stereotypes. One of the pastors from my Asian Bible study group told me, "William, just let this go. Don't make things worse."

Furthermore, I didn't know how things would pan out or how long a music career would last. But I remembered the words of Martin Luther King Jr., who said, "Faith is taking the first step, even when you don't see the whole staircase." I thought about that, and also about the words of a good friend, "This will be your only chance in your lifetime for this kind of opportunity. Do you want to have regrets later on in your life?"

That cinched it for me. I did not want to live with the regret of having passed up a great opportunity. I worked up the courage and I accepted the deal.

The next four years were a whirlwind. I felt like I was living the dream, and I experienced a world that was unattainable for a so-so civil engineering student. I traveled to New York on multiple occasions. I was interviewed on *The Howard Stern Show* and NBC's *Today Show*, and I was on *The Tonight Show* with Jay Leno. And I interviewed with FUSE, one of KOCH Records' partners.

I performed on stage at Wango Tango in front of more than 60,000 people at the Rose Bowl in Pasadena, sharing the stage with The Black Eyed Peas and Janet Jackson. I was shaking and my heart was pounding even as I sang, but I still wasn't nearly as nervous as I had been in that initial *American Idol* audition.

I did a gig in San Diego with nearly 10,000 people. It was a smaller venue that was filled to the gills, and security had to block the entrances to keep people out. It was wild.

I was even invited to promote *Icelandic Idol* in (obviously) Iceland.

But the invitations eventually became fewer and fewer. Not only that, the money was starting to get smaller and smaller. I began to realize that I really needed to save all the money I had earned and go back to school. I had known this was eventually going to happen, and I was ready to find a new direction in my life through education. I was disappointed, but I was also grateful for all of the performance and appearance opportunities that I had received. While I never officially "retired" from my career in entertainment, I put it on the back burner. I still took advantage of opportunities whenever they arose.

In the end, I learned that I wasn't meant to be a student of civil engineering *or* a musical performer. My passion lies elsewhere. I took a long and meandering route to find my purpose in life, but now that I have found it, I feel an overwhelming sense of obligation to share with others the joy of finding one's true calling.

CHAPTER 4

DISCOVERING WHAT YOU WANT

Even as I struggled to maintain my entertainment career, I realized I would need to complete my college education. Because I had always been good at math, I opted to pursue a bachelor's degree in math with the goal of eventually being credentialed to teach.

I had not been in school for more than six years—since my original American audition back in 2004—and I wasn't sure if I was ready to be a college student again. However, this time, I felt more confident compared to when I first started college as a young, immature kid. I could see myself doing whatever it would take to get my degree.

Just as I expected, I did well in classes like geometry and statistics but struggled with classes like advanced linear algebra, which, in fact, was the most difficult barrier I faced in earning my degree. I actually failed the class the first time I took it.

The student-teaching experience was memorable for me in that it was painful. I had good days and I had bad days; it was a roller coaster ride. I was teaching algebra to middle schoolers and high schoolers. The good days were the result of students engaging in hands-on activities; the bad days were when they had to do their classwork quietly on their own. Young people just don't like to sit quietly in a room full of their peers and do math. Go figure.

They also hated homework. My students would find novel ways of avoiding work. They would say, "Mr. Hung, I forgot my pencil; Mr. Hung, I forgot my paper...my book...my homework..." It was always something.

The pressure was beginning to get to me. Halfway through the semester, I had just finished with one of my classes and I found myself alone in the room. I was bombarded with negative thoughts, "Why am I doing this? The students don't want to learn from me. What's the point?" It was overwhelming. I felt hopeless and I broke down in tears.

Although many of the students were not excited about learning math, it turned out that they were very interested to learn about my experience on *American Idol*. Towards the end of the semester, I learned that it was hard for some of the students to take me seriously as their teacher because they perceived me more as an entertainer or a comedian.

To make matters worse, I was discovering to my dismay that

full-time teaching jobs were few and far between. This was back in 2011. The majority of full-time jobs in the teaching profession were for substitutes. If you wanted your own classroom, it was basically "take a number."

So, if you're doing the math, I was: One, trying to teach kids who didn't want to learn, and two, trying to find a job that probably wasn't available. I shared these insights with my parents, explaining that my plans to teach middle and high school math weren't adding up. My mom suggested that I look for jobs with the county government. Why not? It couldn't be worse than banging my head against the wall trying to get middle schoolers to keep their mouths shut and do their work.

The problem I encountered, however, was that most of the jobs I was finding required some sort of prior work experience with the County of Los Angeles, thus creating a catch-22 situation. There was one job, though, that only required a BS in Math or Statistics. The job was for a Statistical Analyst, and I immediately conjured up the vision of crime fighters on a *CSI*-type show or *Criminal Minds*.

As it turned out, the job wasn't quite as sexy as all that. Still, the supervisor who interviewed me knew about my *American Idol* audition. It took two interviews, and when she decided that she would hire me, she asked me why I hadn't put down my experience working in the entertainment industry. I said, "I thought it wasn't relevant to the job I was applying for." She chuckled and said that she was working in the entertainment industry on the side as an assistant for famous singers like Keith Urban. What a coincidence!

Anyway, the actual work was just maintaining and analyzing data quality for crime data. What this meant was that my job was to review a ton of police reports. I know that might sound exciting but it wasn't. On the contrary, it was not only extremely boring and depressing, I found myself up to my ears in a world of murders, rapes, and domestic abuse, among countless other crimes.

As you can imagine, I needed to find something outside of work to do for fun. One day, I saw an online advertisement from the Sheriff's Department about Toastmasters, a nonprofit organization that helps people develop public speaking and leadership skills.

I joined up, initially thinking that I just wanted to talk about something (anything) outside of work, like hobbies, traveling, or other fun stuff. I thought that this was going to be a way to unwind and relax. But I quickly discovered it presented its own measure of seriousness. I was given the opportunity to speak to an entire group of crime analysts about how to start a presentation the proper way. I began the introduction to my speech by saying, "The first words coming out of your mouth can make or break your presentation." So much for fun.

I chose to open boldly because I felt that I needed to get people's attention right away. And what better way to grab their attention than to alert them to the fact that the very first words out of their mouth would have power over everything else that followed.

It was a brief speech, five to seven minutes. The audience said that they really enjoyed it and that the tips were useful. It was just the sort of encouragement I needed.

One year later, I took advantage of the opportunity to do a PowerPoint presentation to recommend the best software to improve productivity for the Statistical Unit that I worked with. Attending the meeting were senior managers, IT staff, and several other colleagues.

I began practicing the presentation two whole months ahead of time, over and over again. I gave the presentation to my Toastmasters group twice simply to get feedback, and they helped me get it right where I wanted it. They gave me feedback on the structure, what to include in my content, and how to deliver the facts in an honest and tactful way. As a result, I nailed it when the time came to present my recommendations, and my now-former supervisor put a letter of commendation into my employee file.

I had no idea at the time that I was heading toward a new career. Once again, my life's journey had taken an unforeseen turn, although I had not yet fully realized that it was happening.

Since then, I've won the coveted "Best Speaker" award frequently at Toastmasters meetings. My group had encouraged me to keep going and to participate in speech contests. The competitive juices began to flow once again, so I gave it a shot.

Toastmasters contests begin at the Club level, then proceed to the Area level, then to the Division level, next to the District level, and then there are the World Championship Semifinals and ultimately the World Championship Finals.

Thus far, I've made it to the Division level twice, and I lost both contests. The second time, in 2017, was particularly disappointing, as I really felt I connected with the audience and received a lot of laughs.

Back in the day, my first album sold more than 200,000 copies worldwide and became Billboard's number-one independent album. In it, I recorded inspirational messages between tracks. The album, optimistic in tone, was aptly titled *Inspiration*. It's where I feel my particular "zone of genius" is. And so, my message remains one of inspiration today—only now, the medium has changed.

CHAPTER 5

CHAMPION BY CHOICE: KEY 1
COMMUNICATE AND SPEAK THE TRUTH

I'm often asked how I was able to acquire fame despite embarrassment on national television. Media critics are especially curious, "How is it possible for someone without true musical talent to succeed in the entertainment industry?"

To this day, I am not sure of the answer to either of those questions. The answers may reside, however, in something that I've heard from my friends and supporters. They all seem to agree on one common trait that I displayed: Authenticity. And if I came across as genuine, it's simply because I actually was.

I did not script my responses nor did I rehearse any potential question-and-answer scenarios. I just reacted to the situation.

If you realize the judges are just playing their roles and doing the job they've been paid (big money) to do, it seems pointless to lose your cool over it. While I might be scoffed at for not having professional-level musical talent, my character was never questioned. I behaved decently and maturely. What audiences saw was the genuine William Hung.

I've always prized authenticity as a key value in my life. And I've learned that *being authentic requires you to be honest with yourself.* As a result, I expect honesty even when it might be difficult. I want to be able to be honest with others, and I also want them to be honest with me.

I think it's fair to say that most of us do want that level of honesty. The problem is that speaking the truth can be difficult. That's why the first key to becoming a Champion by Choice is *communication* that is genuine.

The Criticism Challenge

The most successful professional speakers are not always the most polished public speakers. Their success lies in the fact that they have the courage to stand by their values and viewpoints, no matter how different or out of the mainstream those might be. And they are able to do this because they are willing to be clear about their purpose and their goals.

The number one fear that most people have, as study after study reminds us, is the fear of public speaking. Talking comes so naturally to most of us, so why is it that we're so afraid to stand in front of a room full of others and do something that otherwise is second nature? The root of that fear may well be that we're worried about being judged by our family, friends, or colleagues.

Most of the time, we want to avoid conflict so we might not want to receive criticism or honest feedback.

Tact in the face of criticism can impede authenticity, whether it's conscious or buried somewhere in our psyches, and this often results in euphemisms or indirectness.

For example, when media critics say I am the worst singer or tone deaf, I am not going to just ignore it and let it slide. I might not be the best singer compared to other talented singers but I also know that I am not the worst singer. I would cite how Beyoncé said I was "in tune." I would defend myself by sharing the feedback from my fans that enjoyed listening to my singing.

On the other hand, tact can function as a buffer, allowing you to remain calm when people say difficult things.

There were people who said I didn't deserve to be in the entertainment business. They said I didn't have the same level of talent as most professional singers.

This is a situation I need to handle tactfully. The way I respond is by saying that I consider myself a professional entertainer. My goal as a professional entertainer is to bring joy to other people through entertainment. As long as there are people who enjoy the way I perform and engage with them, I believe I can be successful in my own unique way.

THE PROCRASTINATION CHALLENGE

I remember how I showed up late for one of my performances in Pittsburgh because the flight got there late and I didn't get a chance to do a proper rehearsal. Also, I was overwhelmed by requests for pictures and autographs as soon as I arrived at the event venue. Then, when I performed my signature song "She Bangs," I forgot some of the lyrics from the second verse! I got booed for a while but I was able to recover right before the chorus.

I don't allow that to happen now in any of my performances, appearances, or professional speaking engagements. But back then, I was not as experienced and I could have prevented that problem altogether by making sure I got to the event venue one day earlier. Learning from that event, I now make sure that the event organizer pays the expense for me to get to the event at least one day earlier from West Coast to East Coast and at least two days earlier for international travel.

However, regarding the example above, I could have mentally rehearsed the song beforehand or even on my way there sitting in the car. I didn't do it because I had performed that song thousands of times and I just didn't think I needed to rehearse. I took things for granted.

To combat this deceptive form of procrastination, begin by asking yourself how important that speech or performance is for you. I stopped procrastinating regarding any speech in a professional setting. I realized my brand reputation was on the line. I realized that I always needed to make my very best effort to diligently prepare.

Ultimately, as with most choices in life, it's a matter of prioritizing. If you're conscientious enough to reply in a timely manner to emails, stay in touch with social media contacts, or organize your schedule, you know well enough that you can probably carve out enough time in your week to lay the groundwork for a good speech.

THE SELF-TRUST CHALLENGE

It was not until the beginning of 2017 that I began to take public speaking seriously. Up until then, I was content to have fun speaking at Toastmasters club meetings and participating in speech contests, and I didn't feel any sense of urgency to push myself to the next level. Then one of my friends asked me at the end of 2016 if I had a New Year's resolution. I thought about it and replied that I wanted to inspire the world and that I wanted to help people go after their dreams so they could live a happy and fulfilling life.

That not only remains my resolution; it has become my calling.

It's generally accepted that we give up on our dreams at some point. We attribute this to the insanity-inducing amount of effort required to pursue those dreams. And while somebody may win the lottery, whether literally or metaphorically, it typically takes a lot of hard work to bring a dream to fruition. And putting in that work requires a commitment to achieve a *vision,* which is something that many people don't have. But don't worry, that level of desire is not something you're either born with or you're not; on the contrary, it's something anyone can acquire.

Instead, draw upon current events or your own life experiences to create an authentic connection with your audience. I am not someone who enjoys writing a speech word for word. I know that about myself. Nevertheless, I can still create effective and engaging speeches without worrying about achieving perfection. Your audience doesn't expect perfection from you, but they do expect you to be honest and authentic.

If they've come to hear you, they are going to want *your* perspective on the issue. So, trust yourself and share your truth. Of course, sharing your truth will garner some critics and that's just a fact of life.

In one of my more recent speeches for a local community event, I talked about the need to make "crazy choices" if you want to be successful. I talked about my crazy choices to audition for *American Idol*, to marry girls from a Chinese online dating website, and to go for my dream to become a full-time professional poker player—things I will describe in more detail in the upcoming chapters of this book. My perspective is that my crazy choices are not really that crazy. To me, they are rational and calculated. Of course, there are people who would disagree and that's okay! I received a lot of great feedback for that speech because I provoked emotions in the audience.

Keep in mind that if you don't get criticism, you probably aren't saying anything worth analyzing. If it's helpful, think of criticism as other people's way of opening a dialogue with you and encouraging you to be able to defend the claims you're making.

Also, appreciate that there will be a group of people who are enlightened by your message and are grateful you took the time and had the fortitude to present it.

THE CONCISION CHALLENGE

During my very first professional speech, which I delivered in Malibu, I went on far too long. I remember that the organizer wanted me to talk for about 45 minutes, but I didn't have compelling content for 45 minutes. I could see that people started losing their interest after about 30 minutes. On the very next speaking engagement—the closing keynote speech for the Asian Real Estate Association Installation Gala—I was allowed only 15 minutes. That speech was so much more effective. People were emotionally invested throughout the speech and everyone gave me a standing ovation!

This made me realize that longer speeches are not always better; sometimes, the opposite is true.

Commit yourself to a single key point for people to take home. Our brains are overwhelmed with information from the moment we wake up and check our email to the moment we finally put down the phone at night and crash. Your audience will forget most of what you said. They won't, however, forget how you made them feel—whether that's resentful, inspired, sleepy, energized, ripped off, or valued.

In the second speech, I worked from the premise "One of a Kind," discussing how we Asians are indeed one of a kind and we need to be treated as unique individuals. I focused solely on supporting this key point as the take-away for my audience.

If you've ever listened to a presentation you found confusing or hard to follow, it's likely because the presenter just tried to pack too much into one presentation. No doubt, that person had noble motives and much to share, but unfortunately that's not the ideal way to share information. In fact, by overloading your audience, you're likely to strike them as a pseudo-expert who spent too much time on Wikipedia.

Craig Valentine, 1999's world champion of public speaking (yes, there actually is a competition for such a title), suggests inserting one "key phrase" throughout your speech. While this technique is not mandatory for a compelling speech, it can be a useful tool.

Throughout this book, you will see the key concept "Champion by Choice." This concept is critical, because we need to focus on the *choices* that we make every day and then decide whether they lead us in the direction of success or failure.

CHAPTER 6

YOUR STORIES ARE VALUABLE

*Y*ou have a story to tell. You may or may not know exactly what the central message of that story is or the right way to tell it, but everyone has something to share with the rest of us. If others were gathered to hear you tell them the most important lesson you have learned during your time on this planet, what would you tell them? You probably know that stories help us build connections professionally and personally. As human beings, we love stories. Stories about overcoming adversity, stories about crazy failures, or stories about current events.

The truth is, this world is filled with people waiting for insight from those who have examined their own lives and mined their own experience. It takes courage, of course, to stand in front of an audience and share your message; there's naturally a risk that you might be rejected.

But there's another fear that I want you to consider. It's the fear of watching your dreams slip away because you were afraid of rejection. Now that you have competing fears, ask yourself which is the greater one. Are you more afraid of disapproval or of failing to realize your potential? If it's the former, maybe it's time to let go of those dreams. If, however, it's the latter, there's hope of turning those dreams into reality—and ultimately exploring and realizing your potential.

I know, because I've been there myself as a young man who dramatically bombed his audition on *American Idol* in front of a national television audience—a bomb that has been viewed more than five million times on *YouTube*. But what looked like a humiliating failure actually turned out to be my greatest opportunity.

As a result of that "failed" attempt, I got a taste of fame. I got a recording contract. I got parts in a movie and on the critically acclaimed television series *Arrested Development*. None of that would have happened had I not taken a chance and "failed."

I could have taken a different route. It would have been much easier to simply stay in bed the next day, unplug the phone, and wallow in self-pity.

But instead, I embraced what happened. Then I accepted

each opportunity that came my way and made the best of it. I cannot take back my *American Idol* audition and the negative publicity that came with it. Some people will love me, and some people will hate me; I feel like I am unintentionally very polarizing. It's based on other people's first impression of me and what they read from the internet or the public news. I'm inspired by the words Oscar Wilde wrote, "What seems to us bitter trials are often blessings in disguise."

Taking a big risk and "failing" publicly is my story. I've met many others who have had negative experiences and found inspiration in mine—such as Darren Tay, 2016 Toastmasters World Champion of Public Speaking from Singapore, who had to deal with bullying for many years during his childhood. The knowledge that I can bring others hope brings me joy.

I have leveraged my story to become a speaker, which allows me to share my message with people I would otherwise never have encountered. I've spoken to companies, associations, and schools.

Then it didn't take long before I found other ways that I could make valuable use of my story, such as helping other speakers develop their signature talk, improve their delivery, and become more impactful. I've worked to become a public speaking coach and I help entrepreneurs and professionals to shift their perspectives, to see the opportunities in failure by changing their mindset. I aim to help others discover self-confidence so they feel empowered to overcome their fears, realize their dreams, and take risks.

I benefit enormously from such work. I am extremely grateful for the roller coaster that brought me here so my story might inspire people to live the life they really want.

You, too, have a story to tell. If you do not want to have suffered humiliation or defeat in vain, take that failure and turn it on its head. Learn from it and share it with others. It just might be your greatest victory. In the next chapter, I'll explain how.

CHAPTER 7

LEVERAGING FAILURES AND FRUSTRATIONS

Although we don't necessarily like to admit it, failures and frustrations happen all the time. They might be as simple as getting stuck in traffic, dealing with lousy customer service, or being unhappy with your current job.

Think about where your thoughts go in such moments. Don't they go deeper than just that morning commute, unhelpful customer representative, or boring office task? In those situations, it's common to question your whole existence, as in, "I waste an entire week of my life every year sitting in my car," "I hate being treated like a number," or "This isn't where I thought I'd be at this stage in my life."

You may be thinking to yourself as you read this, "William is doing great and he's making loads of money in the entertainment business. Of course he's happy. He's living the dream."

While those are not the exact words I hear from people whom I meet, that's the gist. And while I am certainly a glass-is-half-full kind of guy, I know all about failures and frustrations, both large and small.

Not all of my failures have been as public as my *American Idol* audition. For instance, I've gone through two divorces. In the spirit of rapport-building, I'll share some details.

I met my first wife on a Chinese dating website. I was 29 or 30 years old at the time and naive enough to believe in "love at first sight." I eventually went to China and met her in person, and I told myself right then that I was in love. I married her a week later. My friends would say that I needed to know someone for two or three years before getting married. However, I had been chatting with her online and via video conferences, and I thought it would be hard to see her again in person because I would need to fly back and forth between the US and China. I felt pressured to make a quick decision, and the first time I hung out with her in person, I felt great having her by my side. So, I decided to trust my gut instincts.

Unfortunately, it didn't work out. Within 10 months, we divorced. I had never dreamt that our marriage would fail so I didn't have her sign a prenuptial agreement. That turned out to be a rather expensive failure but a valuable lesson. I realized how the long time-gap between our marriage in China and the time we finally got to see each other in person in the US was really bad. We had definitely tried to stay in touch using instant messaging and video conferencing but by the time she arrived in the US, the lust for a romantic relationship was already gone.

Wife number two was, like me, living in the Los Angeles area. So this time, I made sure to get to know my would-be bride better before popping the question: Six months, to be precise. We would hang out for lunch and dinner, go to the parks, go to movies, go whale watching, and do other fun things together. Then after about three months, my parents pressured me to get married; they really wanted grandchildren. Having learned from my first marriage, I did not make the decision to marry my second wife based on that. I decided to marry her because I saw that she was a kind, loving person who genuinely cared about me. That marriage was full of ups and downs, and it lasted two and a half years.

Both women were young and attractive. It would be fair to say that I was preoccupied with outside appearances. I failed to explore their life vision and values.

That second divorce is still a painful subject. My parents were mean to my wife. They were overprotective of me and they always said that I was right and she was wrong—on issues like eating out, finances, and household duties. I was hoping somehow that we could live together as one family because as Chinese, we value harmony. But my mom would even say to me at times that she was a "witch" manipulating my mind so I would not listen to my parents! My wife cried and said that she was moving out, with or without me. I finally sided with her and we moved out together after a year and a half of living with my parents. But the damage to our relationship was already done; I could not repair the relationship even after we moved.

After my divorce, I spiraled into a depression. Apart from work, which I would have quit if I had the luxury to do so, I felt too fatigued to do anything except play video games, play poker, and watch sports. If unplugging from reality had been an option, I'd have signed up.

In early 2017, a friend of mine cheered me up and brought me out of my months-long stupor. She was one of my friends from Toastmasters and she said that I had been a role model for her. She said that I had inspired her to constantly improve her public speaking and that it seemed very uncharacteristic of me to be in a slump and unmotivated to do anything about it. Then we talked about my very first album *Inspiration* and how it had short motivational messages in between the songs. She said she was one of my biggest fans and still listened to my albums.

Somehow, this gave me an insight: Maybe I could inspire people by becoming an inspirational speaker. I knew I was not the only guy who had gone through a divorce. A lot of relationships fail, and thus the subject is quite universal. So, rather than wallow in my own misery, I took that failure and I shared in humorous fashion the wisdom that I had gleaned from it. I figured it could help others who had dealt with, or were currently dealing with, the pain from their own failed attempts at building a long-lasting relationship.

Don't let your particular failures and frustrations stand in the way of sharing your story. Others have been there, or are there, or will be there, and they need to hear your message of inspiration.

CHAPTER 8

CHAMPION BY CHOICE: KEY 2
CONTEXT

If you want to succeed at creating the life you want, you will need to make hard choices and be willing to accept both the favorable and unfavorable results. You decide the choices you make, but the results are often beyond your control.

At the end of 2008, I encountered a difficult choice. It was one of the hardest decisions I have ever had to make. My entertainment career had begun to decline and I had to decide whether to keep hoping for performance and appearance opportunities or to finish college and find a stable job.

I'll never know for sure what might have come my way if I'd kept waiting for my entertainment career to lift off, but there are some risks that aren't worth taking. If the entertainment choice didn't work out, I would have nothing to fall back on, so I chose to finish school and find a steady job.

It's not as glamorous as being a recording star, I know, but I wanted to hone my other skills and find a way to make a more reliable living. Although taking a day job is rare for celebrities, it is actually very common for them to build their own business and find other streams of income. This is because it is very unlikely that people will receive reliable long-term income from just doing performances, movie roles, and/or appearances.

That's why I chose to take the job at the Los Angeles County Sheriff's Department as a Statistical Analyst, thus leveraging my knowledge of math and statistics.

After a couple of years at the Sheriff's Department and a dozen interviews, I finally earned a promotion and changed departments. I was made administrative assistant at the Department of Public Health. I knew I would be working on a greater variety of tasks and projects as compared with my previous job, so I was excited. Along the way, I had considered giving up and blaming my circumstances. But I didn't because I knew I needed to keep advancing my career, and I decided to keep working to improve my interview skills.

I had discovered that it was my interviewing skills that were holding me back because when I watched samples of how other professionals sold themselves in their interviews, I could see that I had been doing things all wrong. Rather than trying to *oversell* my skill sets, I needed to change my perspective and look at the advertised job from the manager's point of view. *How could he benefit from hiring me?*

I eventually focused on *how I could solve problems for the organization*. I thought about *why* they needed to hire someone for the position. In this case, it turned out that the division needed to build a new contract database using Microsoft Access, something with which I had plenty of experience. When I discovered that, I was able to land the job.

Am I satisfied now that I have that job? No. Would I be writing this book if I were? I'll never be content with a regular nine-to-five job because I believe I am meant for something more. I see myself as someone who will inspire other people through speaking and coaching. It feels like my higher calling.

If the first key to becoming a "Champion by Choice" is *communication*, the second is *context*. We're often told that we need to "see the big picture." But what does that mean? I propose that it means taking ownership of the choices you make. And in making those choices, you can either be self-determined or other-determined.

"Self-determined" means that you determine your thoughts, feelings, actions, behaviors, and emotions. "Other-determined" means someone or something besides yourself is determining your thoughts, feelings, actions, behaviors, and emotions.

Even knowing this, it's still difficult to live a self-determined life. So, how do we do it?

The first way in which you can be self-determined is by taking responsibility for outcomes you don't have control over. While that may sound paradoxical on its surface, it isn't. In making your choice, you must learn to own the results, whether they are positive or negative.

My decision to go back to school to finish my degree and look for a stable job may or may not have been the best decision at the time. It's possible that I would have been better off leveraging my celebrity fame by looking for an agent to continue working in the entertainment industry. Or perhaps I could have gone into sales or started my own business. However, when I made my decision to be more conservative with my life, I accepted that I wouldn't suddenly get rich. I also wouldn't risk going broke.

The *second way* in which you can be self-determined is by valuing your time. If you don't choose to place a high value on your time, others won't either. Outside forces will encroach on your time, making it difficult for you to chart your own course and follow your own path.

I often find myself wasting time surfing the internet and checking out social media to see what is happening with my friends. I say yes to too many networking events. I still waste time with video games or computers to avoid tasks I don't want to do.

Becoming self-determined also requires you to value your choices regarding things that might seem trivial. Things like what you eat each day, how you get to work, and who you spend your time with. Without a bird's-eye view of your life, it can be hard to actually determine what is trivial and what is important.

Thirdly, by valuing even minor choices that you make each day, you're developing the good habit of being conscious and intentional with making your choices.

The biggest choice I had to make after my *American Idol* audition was whether to take a chance with the entertainment dream or walk away.

I knew I didn't have the same talent as some of the stars who had succeeded on that show. I couldn't sing and dance like Carrie Underwood. But I also knew that I had just been given a showbiz break that doesn't come around often, so I thought it was worth testing out. I found my answer when a classmate from my civil engineering class counseled me, saying, "This is your once-in-a-lifetime opportunity. If you don't take advantage of this, you'll regret it for the rest of your life."

Deciding to take advantage of that opportunity shaped the rest of my life. It stopped me from living with deep-seated regret.

When I was performing, I got to travel to many places around the world, making a name for myself and connecting with people from all walks of life.

I chose to see what would happen, even though I could not make anyone buy my records or show up to see my performances. I could not control the outcome of my decision. But I took responsibility for it.

Reflecting again on my experience working in the entertainment industry, I finally feel empowered to take steps to get out of a job I no longer enjoy. Just as before, when I left school to pursue a singing career, it will take courage. I may fail, but I can live with that. But I wouldn't be able to live with the regret of not having tried because I was too afraid.

So, ask yourself honestly if you're satisfied with where you're at in your life right now. But don't stop there; consider whether you'll be happy five years from now on the same course. And how about farther down the road?

If, in fact, you are not totally satisfied with your life right now, don't worry. You're not alone. You have the ability to make choices that will affect your future. And if you're unhappy, that's a good motivation to make smart choices.

Consider establishing a vision for yourself and setting reasonable goals to achieve it. Look long term, but don't overlook the milestones along the way so that you can see your own progress and determine if your decisions are resulting in positive or negative consequences.

I do this in my own life. My goal at this point is to earn a good living from professional speaking and playing poker. Later, I intend to pivot to investing in low-risk endeavors, such as low-cost index funds and real estate.

That's where I'm trying to get to, which is better than where I am now. I'm not relying on luck in the long term. There is obviously luck in the short term, but I am confident that skill will be the deciding factor in the long term. I'm taking what I believe to be smart, calculated risks and making decisions that I am accountable for. Come what may, I'll sleep well knowing I did my best.

CHAPTER 9

CHANGING YOUR PERCEPTION ABOUT RISK

I magine standing on top of a three-story building with a large swimming pool below. On the count of three, you're going to jump. How does that make you feel? Terrified? Excited? Or is this exercise just too far removed from your reality that you're thinking to yourself, "That's never going to be a place I'd ever find myself in."

"Risk" is defined as a situation involving exposure to danger. Whether you like it or not, risk is all around you. Some of those risks you see; most you don't. No matter how safely you try to live your life, you can't escape risk.

It makes no sense to dwell on risks that can't be avoided. No amount of worry will impact the outcome. For risks that *can* be minimized or mitigated, however, devote what you think is an appropriate amount of attention to them. For me, that equation looks something like, "What is at stake and how much will my decision matter?" If there's a lot on the line and my decision will weigh heavily on the outcome, that's something worthy of my time. Whereas, if there's very little to be won or lost and what I do won't have a serious impact, it's not worth stewing over. It's between those two extremes where what is an appropriate amount of concern becomes fuzzier.

One of the difficult decisions I need to think about right now is how I want to invest my hard-earned money. I already have a lot of expenses like a mortgage, car insurance, and loans that I have to pay, but what should I do with the money I have been saving up each month? I could consider options trading, or putting it into index funds, or stocks, or investing in something else.

The bulk of your decision-making time should, therefore, be devoted to higher-stakes decisions that will have a significant impact. We make these every day. They might include the way we treat people and what we put into our bodies. There are easily foreseeable consequences to these decisions, but that doesn't mean you need to worry. It just means you should be conscious of them, make your choices, and take responsibility for the outcomes.

Many people assume that the biggest risk I've taken in my life was the *American Idol* audition. For some, it's the fact that I left Berkeley to pursue an entertainment career. But the truth is, what I'm doing now is without a doubt the most critical hand I've played to date: giving up a solid government job to become a full-time professional poker player.

I started playing poker back in 2004 because I needed something fun to do during my downtime between my various appearances as an entertainer. I only started taking poker seriously in September 2017. I had tried very hard to get my speaking business to replace my income from my government job, but it became clear that I couldn't get enough paid speaking engagements to sustain myself. And I wasn't able to get many clients who wanted coaching in the area of public speaking. Meanwhile, I had previously won some money playing poker, so why not give that a try?

"Are you crazy?" my parents asked. "Do you realize what you are giving up?"

Well, there was the paycheck every two weeks, health insurance, and my parents' roof over my head. Yes, I knew very well what the ante was.

I also knew how much money I could make. I knew *I'd* be in control of my schedule instead of the County of Los Angeles. I knew that with a large enough stake, I could transition into a career as a full-time investor.

In other words, I knew the risks and I knew the rewards. I had done my homework and I was ready to commit to a decision. *And* I was ready to live with the consequences.

Those are the same calculations you, or anyone else, needs to make when it comes to big decisions in your life.

Oscar-winner Geena Davis, who has a history of choosing bold acting roles, says, "If you risk nothing, then you risk everything."

I take from that the idea that if I'm afraid to venture away from my nine-to-five job, I'm risking whatever more meaningful and exciting life might be awaiting me.

I want to have the opportunity to travel to places I haven't been to yet. I want to work smarter instead of harder. I want to have more money to start my own family and to have more time to spend with my future wife and children.

That sentiment doesn't ring true, however, for my conservative-minded parents. My dad is almost 70 and my mom isn't far behind. They're close to retirement. They own condominiums, which will help to generate much-needed passive income that will serve them well when their working income stops. Obviously, it wouldn't make any sense for them to cash out those condos and take the money to Las Vegas.

I absolutely respect my folks' decision to play it safe; it makes total sense. But I am still relatively young with what I hope is a lot of life left to live. I can't afford to sit around and simply hope to inherit those condos one day. Instead, I need to make my own fortune and learn how to invest it properly. We each must make our own decisions and live with the consequences.

THREE LESSONS FROM POKER

I started playing poker in 2004. Since then, the game has taught me many lessons. There are three that I'd like to share, and which you can apply in your own life.

1. ***Luck***. Like poker, life has elements of both skill and luck. Regarding the things we care most about, such as our relationships, health, or money, *our* decisions only carry so much weight. Don't get me wrong—we can make very good or very bad choices, but other people's decisions will also affect us, and life happens…

   No matter how much I tried to make my marriage work (either one, take your pick), there was another person in that relationship who was making decisions. I made some bad decisions, and any one of them could have led to a breakup. Compound that with the other person's bad decisions and you have a recipe for disaster. But even had we both made wiser choices, outside factors would also have played a role in determining whether the marriage prevailed. Had one of us fallen in love with someone else, for example, that would have factored into the equation.

   Also, no matter how healthily we may try to live, one can still become seriously ill. A car accident, God forbid, could leave you maimed tomorrow. As the Bible says, the rain falls on the just and the unjust alike. One unforeseen catastrophe can undo all the spinach you ever ate and all the laps you ever ran.

As for money, it is not something that is ever easy to control; the stock market is volatile, and no investment is ever without risk. The initial market boom of cryptocurrency is a good example. At its peak in December of 2017, a single Bitcoin was valued at more than $19,000 USD. Just 12 months later, that same Bitcoin was worth $4,000 USD, a little more than 20 percent of its value the year before. Were the people who initially got rich on Bitcoin geniuses? Were the ones who lost money idiots? No, not necessarily, and certainly not as a matter of fact. The point is that markets can be bullish or bearish, and a good deal of luck is necessary to get the timing right as to when to get in and when to get out.

As I've said, cards are my preferred path to wealth and the following are examples learned at the poker table. I know firsthand how fickle the cards can be. In October 2018, I was making a good deal of money from both cash games and tournaments. I felt pretty good about myself as a player, and I began planning my retirement from my day job. And then came November. I finished the month in the black, but it was much harder than I thought and not the reliable operation I had anticipated. I had grossly overestimated my skill.

I finally had my first losing month in January 2019. It was very frustrating because I was doing well with cash games but I wanted to go for a big score by winning a poker tournament. For some reason, I thought that making $8,000 to $10,000 a month was not enough for me. I wanted to get lucky by making $150,000 or more in a few days. Poker tournaments have very high variance. I could certainly get lucky and win more than $150,000 in a few days, but usually I will lose the tournament entry fee and this can happen more than 80 percent of the time. During my entire trip, I lost my entry fee without getting anything back for most of the entries. As a result, I gave away all of my profit that I had worked so hard to get in the course of the month (over $8,000), and I got just one small cash out for about $1,400 after a $400 entry fee.

I don't want to sound like a fatalist here but whether you're experiencing a winning streak or you're in a downward spiral, it's important to ask yourself how much of it is *your* doing and how much of it is just out of your hands. Generally, our egos tend to downplay luck as a factor when we're winning but blame it when we're losing.

2. ***Quantification***. When I'm playing poker, I can't just assume that an opponent is bluffing. Doing so is a surefire way to lose money. That's because poker is a

game of probabilities and precision. Therefore, I train myself to think in terms of numbers. If something is probable, it means there's anywhere from a 50 percent to a 99 percent chance of it occurring.

So, to apply this to my life, I try to consider whether an event is probable, then try to zoom in to determine *how* probable, and place a best-bet percentage on what that might be. It can be as simple as making sure I don't miss my next flight from Los Angeles to New York. Instead of saying I'll probably make it if I get to the airport one hour before departure time, I can say that if I get to the airport one hour before departure time, I expect to make the flight 98 percent of the time. I usually pack as lightly as possible, with a 20-inch carry-on and no checked luggage. It typically takes less than 30 minutes to get through security, which gives me a cushion of 30 minutes to find my gate and do whatever I need to do before boarding the plane.

Of course, I don't mind giving myself *more* additional time to eat, relax, and play on my computer. If a flight is extremely critical to me, however, such as an international flight, a 98 percent probability of being on time is not good enough. I need to be certain to make that flight; in other words, I need to turn that probability into a certainty, which in numerical terms is 100 percent.

By thinking about big decisions in numerical terms, you'll be able to prioritize your time and values with more precision. You'll also have a greater sense of what role you play in the equation and what role other factors can play, and then you can adjust accordingly.

3. *Intuition.* The third lesson that I've learned from the tables is intuition. You have no doubt heard it said about poker that "You don't play the cards, you play the man." Ultimately, poker is about knowing the person across the table from you. Maybe that person has better cards than you—maybe not. The winner isn't necessarily the one who holds the best cards; it's the one who holds the best cards after all the betting is done.

The good news is that you can *develop* intuition. The bad news is that you develop it through trial and error. Intuition, or "your gut," will eventually become very good at making snap judgments. If you pay attention to it over time, you can learn to trust it. That's a skill. Do you feel an ulcer coming on every time you consider taking a certain friend's financial advice? That may literally be your gut trying to warn you.

Before you decide you implicitly trust your gut, however, ask yourself how it's been doing lately. Did that last hunch you had pay off, or are you still paying the price for it? What has been its win-loss percentage? If it's 50-50, you might as well just flip a coin.

Unless and until you have crafted a finely tuned sense of intuition, it's best to reserve it for life's smaller decisions, like who to invite to a dinner party or where to sit in a movie theater. When it comes to the hard choices, your best bet is deliberate, careful analysis, and a good night's sleep.

CHAPTER 10

MAXIMIZE YOUR IMPACT

I used to have a hard time saying no. When I first began working as a professional entertainer in 2004, I agreed to fly on a red-eye flight from Los Angeles to New York immediately following an exhausting performance. I was set to perform the next morning on NBC's *Today Show* at Times Square. It was a huge gig, so I was willing to endure a little discomfort to do it.

A little discomfort would have been fine. What I endured was the flight from hell. It was turbulent throughout, preventing me from getting my 40 winks. Then shortly before I was to take the stage, I suffered a nasty nosebleed and nearly passed out. A doctor backstage checked me out and said I had low blood pressure.

I still went out there and performed, and I survived. I did my thing. But what if I hadn't? What if I had breached the contract? What if I had fainted backstage? Or onstage? These thoughts have haunted me ever since. After this experience, I made a promise to myself—I vowed to never knowingly put myself in harm's way again.

I can't blame anyone but myself for being in that situation. I agreed to do it. It was my fault I wound up in poor shape. It wasn't the first time either; it was just the straw that broke the camel's back.

I was making a lot of money at that time, but I was so stressed both physically and mentally that I had to finally ask myself, "Is it worth it?"

Those cash-versus-pain decisions came up when I needed to pick which performances, appearances, interviews, and speaking opportunities to pursue. Just like in poker, you must decide which hands are worth playing and which are best folded. And just like in poker, the best strategy is to fold whenever you're low on the table. Let me translate: If you're unlikely to succeed given the facts that you know, you're probably going to fail. Occasionally, you may get lucky, but that's not a viable long-term plan if you want to keep your money.

When in doubt, rely on the 80/20 Rule. Don't go in on every hand. Instead, save your resources for golden opportunities so that you can maximize your impact when the cards are in your favor. That way you can marshal your forces to make a strategic strike.

The question you need to ask yourself is the same one I had

to ask, "Is it worth it?" Weigh the value of what you'll receive against the toll of what it will cost you. If you're like me, you have probably said to yourself, "Damn it! I should have said no." Then you kick yourself.

I'm certainly not alone in trying to shoulder more than I am capable of bearing. You've probably experienced it also. We live in a dog-eat-dog world in which employers will try to get as much out of their workforce as they can. There's nothing wrong with maximizing human potential but you can sap the life out of people that way. Like I pointed out earlier, it's up to *you* to preserve your self-determination. It's *your* responsibility.

In Chinese culture, and in the larger East Asian culture, saying yes is a sign of respect and speaks to your character. It says you are a hard worker who makes contributions and sacrifices for something greater than yourself. When that concept is woven into the very fabric of a society, it's almost unconscionable to think otherwise.

But consider what Warren Buffett, who by any measure is one of the most successful men in the world, had to say on the subject, "The difference between successful people and *really* successful people is that really successful people say no to almost everything."

After my difficult performance on the *Today Show*, I now limit myself to traveling only four times a month and only once per week. I might be leaving money on the table but to help offset that, I've substantially raised my quote. Now, I don't feel obliged to say yes to every performance or interview opportunity that arises. I only need to take the gigs that interest me most. Or, to put it in poker terms, I don't feel the need to play a hand unless I'm holding a pair of jacks or better.

If you're thinking to yourself, "Well, of course, you have that luxury, William, you're successful enough that you can afford it."

Not true. Even after my entertainment career started to decline in 2008, I didn't drastically decrease my appearance fees. Instead, I used the time I had to finish my education and start a new career working for LA County.

When I first began my professional speaking business in 2017, I felt I needed to "pay my dues," which for me meant speaking for nominal fees or for nothing at all. For the first six to nine months, I just accepted it. To make matters worse, I was running around like a chicken with its head cut off. I felt physically and mentally burned out. I wasn't helping myself, obviously, but I probably wasn't doing much to help my clients, either.

One day during that year, I learned I didn't have to operate that way. One of my mentors told me I needed to value myself more or else others wouldn't value me at the level I believed I deserved. The lesson goes beyond speaking fees.

Once I began to think about my contribution in those terms, I stopped accepting all offers below $4,500. I might make exceptions if I see that there is a clear and tangible benefit that will help grow my business, such as key connections to other paid speaking opportunities or the potential to get coaching clients for public speaking.

I don't want to give you the impression that I'm only interested in money. I'm not. I'm a passionate ambassador for Toastmasters, which doesn't pay me a dime; I just really like their mission. It's a unique platform where people get to speak, receive feedback, and provide feedback to others.

I have a rate that meets my needs. When someone pays it, they are showing me that they respect my time and my message at that price. It means they value me as much as I value myself. And by earning enough money from my business engagements, I have the luxury of choosing to do some work *pro bono*. As we all know, it feels good to give something back.

CHAPTER 11

Champion by Choice: Key 3 Connect with the Right People

It's easy to see the fame I acquired from *American Idol* as mere luck. Make no mistake, there was a lot of luck involved. And had I done nothing in the wake of it, that luck may have been of the bad variety. As it happens, however, I found a certain degree of success in the entertainment industry because of a little luck and some savvy choices on my part.

I connected with the right people at the right time as I navigated my journey. As I mentioned earlier, I would not have been able to get on the show had I not found my way through the preliminary rounds. A producer on the show thought that I was a good fit so she pushed me through. That producer turned out to be an integral figure in my story.

And now to return to the final key to becoming a "Champion by Choice." The third key is *connecting*. Connecting with the right people will allow you to improve both your business and your personal life. Your network serves not only as a lead source for new business but as a sounding board, a support system, and a news source. It's not free, though; it requires maintenance to keep it working.

Most of all, perhaps, a connection cannot be one-sided. I had a Filipina friend that seemed to always take advantage of my generosity. Every time I saw her, she wanted me to help her with something. I like giving to people, but at some point, I had to draw a line in the sand. When she finally asked me to commit to her expensive eight-week coaching program, I knew it was time to bail out and I stopped connecting with her.

Reciprocity means you play both roles. Sometimes you need a favor, and sometimes you grant a favor. If that evens out over time, chances are you'll have developed a solid connection. And that's a valuable thing to have in this world. If strategically managed and nurtured, your network can become a valuable part of your personal brand arsenal, allowing you to enhance your reputation and advance your agenda.

Unless you were raised in the wild by wolves, you already have a network. For our purposes, it's important we distinguish between that catchall connotation and a more specific, useful notion of the word. When I refer to your network, I am talking about it in terms of the strategic sense in which you actively target, cultivate, and maintain mutual alliances.

The way in which you build this network is probably the same way in which you chose your social media friends: You start with the sphere of people you know best and develop it incrementally in concentric circles outward. In practice, this might mean beginning with your nuclear family, extending next to your closest friends, then coworkers or colleagues, perhaps extended family next, followed by contacts in your alumni, professional, or philanthropic organizations, or maybe people you meet at social functions, business mixers, or other meet-and-greet events.

I recommend treating this collection of potential allies like a living, breathing organism. Being incarnate, your network requires proper care and feeding, which should come in the form of regular communication, the exchange of favors, and other helpful interactions. Below are some tips that will help you keep your network functioning at its fullest potential.

Sincerity. Be genuine in your communications so people in your network know that they are valued. Nobody wants to feel like they're being contacted simply as a maintenance requirement or chore. Each person in your network is unique and worthy of respect and appreciation.

Honesty. When someone comes to you for help but you're unable to provide it, say so. Don't fake it, half-ass it, or offer something you know to be of little value. That other person has others in their network they can turn to, but if they waste their time and resources following your advice, you're hurting rather than helping.

Boundaries. Understand the limits of each individual contact in your network. Are you asking for an introduction or are you asking for a kidney? Is the favor you're asking commensurate with the relationship you have with that person? You might be fine asking a lifelong friend for a $1,000 loan, but that request would probably be very uncomfortable for someone you met at a Chamber of Commerce pancake breakfast the week before.

Initiative. Be on the lookout for ways to provide value in your relationships. Don't just wait to be asked. If you come across a news article that you think would benefit a contact, share it. If you can facilitate a connection between contacts you feel could mutually benefit by meeting, host them. It's poor form to only show up when you need something. If you make enough deposits to the bank of goodwill, it's okay to write a check now and then.

Accessibility. Talk is cheap. If you position yourself as a person who is there for others, you need to be there when others come calling. If you're someone who always seems to be busy or otherwise engaged whenever help is sought, you'll develop a reputation as a flake. There's probably not anything more useless in a network than that. If you have flakes in your network, consider culling them.

Gratitude. In addition to reciprocating when appropriate, be sure to express your thankfulness whenever anyone helps or even attempts to help you. And to apply an earlier tip, be sincere about it. A handwritten "thank-you" note or a gift basket is worth a lot more than an email.

Respect. Your full network, if it's going to be effective, should include an array of people across a variety of spectrums. And given that it is diverse, it's important to show respect to every person in it. Don't post something that someone in your network might find offensive (better still, don't post anything that anyone would find offensive). Avoid it if only because it alienates you from others. Extend respect even to your competitors; it will provide you with the drive to continually try to improve. Respect is at the heart of long-lasting relationships and it is the basis for a free society.

Our communities have expanded beyond anything former generations would recognize. But just because you have thousands of "friends" on Facebook doesn't mean you have a friend in this world in any meaningful sense. Understand the difference between people who care about you and people who pretend to watch and like your kid's dance recital video. Friendship requires time, effort, and sacrifice from both parties. If you have relationships like that in your network, you have built powerful alliances.

CHAPTER 12

HOW TO ADD VALUE TO OTHERS

When I got my first taste of fame, a friend told me, "If you charge a dollar every time you take a picture with someone, you'll be a millionaire!" I don't know how much I'd have made over the last 15 years but even if it was a million dollars, who wants to do that? The fact is, the more people take photographs with me, the better off I am. When they do, they will naturally spread those around to their friends and post the pictures on their social media networks. It's good for my brand. More importantly, it's something I can do to show my gratefulness to my fans, who are largely responsible for my success as an entertainer.

Being available for photo opportunities with fans hasn't given me the same sphere of influence as, say, Usher. That's not going to happen. But, as a result, I've developed a larger fan base than many other former *American Idol* contestants.

I used to get scared when a group of people would confront me to get a picture.

I will never forget how a bunch of girls wanted to take pictures with me as I was waiting for my flight to go to Houston. Those girls mobbed me! Not maliciously but they still freaked me out because I had never encountered that situation before. I remember I still had plenty of time before my flight so I agreed to take pictures with all of them, one by one. There were 20 to 30 girls total. They were all Caucasian and they were mostly teenagers or young adults.

A friend in the public relations business explained to me that I needed to embrace it, "Don't try to run away; be nice to them. If you can't be gracious even to the people who support you, where's that going to get you?"

You don't have to be even borderline famous to have support- ers. As I said in the previous chapter, we all have a network. Think about the things you can do to add value to those people. Maybe it's not taking a photo with them but the phi- losophy behind it is the same: make yourself available.

A lot of celebrities, especially A-list celebrities, are not going to want to take pictures with fans in random public places. If they attend an event where they expect to be photographed with fans, such as a VIP meet and greet, they expect to do so. That's fine, but they're not obliged to take photos with fans on the street. It's important to remember that choosing to take photos is just that, a choice.

Offering something of value to your supporters is good practice, regardless of what comes from it. That said, some of those supporters will reciprocate and provide you with something of value. Most of them probably won't, but that's not the point. The benefits you'll derive from the few who do will be worth it.

Let me clarify what I mean by "adding value." Doing something for people that should naturally be part of the product, job, or service *does not add value*. Adding value requires that you give people something they want but don't expect. Again, taking photos with fans is not in the job description so when a celebrity does agree to take one, that person is offering something extra.

In providing something of value, I believe it's important to strike the right balance. Carol Cox, a mentor of mine, says it's imperative to have your own unique framework for how to work with clients. She encourages entrepreneurs to give potential clients enough information to build trust. However, if you give away too much information, then your potential clients will solve their problems without you!

Now you're probably saying to yourself, "How is it possible for me to hold information back while still coming across as someone who genuinely adds value?" The key is to solve the problems that are so complicated that they require cooperation. Simple example: Ice. Selling ice is a dead-end job. Anyone can cool water to below freezing—there's no demand for artisanal ice. But there is a need for freezer repair. You can teach in a series of *YouTube* videos how to fix your own freezer. A few people will watch and make the repair. A lot more people will see you successfully fixing a freezer and decide, "That's too complicated for me—but *that* person knows how to fix my freezer and I'm going to hire them!"

A less simple example is how Carol Cox built her expertise in developing signature talks for female entrepreneurs. She is very transparent about her methods. She even allows visitors to her site to download PDFs, free of charge, and create their own signature talk. They can do so if they're willing to follow her step-by-step process and then share the feedback they get from the people in their network.

She sees it as a win-win situation. She's able to offer her visitors something of value (her process), and in return, that person shares something of value (feedback). It also allows her to establish rapport and prove that she knows what she's doing.

Cox can help a person create a signature talk in about four or five hours of actual work time. There are some preparations beforehand and some editing afterwards, as well as an intensive three-hour, one-on-one session to put the pieces of the puzzle together, so to speak. Without the expertise of someone like Cox, that work might take exponentially longer, or people might just discard their talk altogether due to frustration or self-doubt.

When I mentor speakers in Toastmasters, I follow a method similar to that of Cox. I seek to help someone reverse-engineer a speech by initially determining what goals that person wants to achieve. Once they establish those goals, we can focus on the stories that fit into the speech. I try to remove the guesswork for others so they feel secure that what they have to say is important, compelling, and to the point. An awkward or embarrassing first speech can cripple a person's confidence, which can deter them from getting back out there.

As you think about how you can provide value to others, consider the area or areas in which you have some degree of expertise. We all have something to offer. Maybe your job provides you with specialization in a certain field, maybe a discipline you studied in college could be put to good use to help others, or maybe you have a hobby that lends itself to the task.

The point is, you have something that other people need. By discovering what that something is, you can add value to the lives of others. That's how you build fruitful, long-term relationships.

CHAPTER 13

TREATING PEOPLE WITH RESPECT

I think it's worth acknowledging the bitter truth: the world can be a cruel place.

You've probably experienced some degree of mean-spiritedness if you've ever been on the internet. Perhaps, it's the anonymity that the medium provides in the same way that road rage offers the isolation of one's personal vehicle, but it's clear we are living in an age in which people feel empowered to treat others with impunity.

If the Golden Rule was ever in effect, it certainly isn't now.

I feel I came of age when incivility and open hostility made their public debut, and it seems reasonable to say that much of the blame belongs to my ticket to fame: *American Idol.*

The judge-empaneled talent show served as a vehicle not only to admire performers with singing ability but to publicly shame those without it, and no one more so than yours truly. In fact, it's quite possible that my performance, even in the third season of the program, marked something of a cultural zeitgeist—a turning point in which we were all given license to play Simon Cowell in our own lives with the power to sit back and scorn the people around us.

While there were three judges on the show, Cowell was the unquestioned star because he was the harshest and most abusive in his criticism. To put it another way, he was a bully. And that's what people tuned in for. The secret sauce was schadenfreude (described in the dictionary as "a feeling of pleasure or satisfaction when something bad happens to someone else"). The producers understood, however, that nobody wants to admit to such shameful feelings; they couldn't have a show that was devoted solely to laughing at others. Instead, they had to conceal it in something aspirational, which allowed viewers to appreciate the vocally gifted. It also made for a striking contrast.

When a TV star is rewarded for basically being a meanie, it justifies that behavior in the audience. The network essentially set a standard regarding bullying. That, in my opinion, seeded the landscape for millions of Simon Cowell wannabes.

As I've said before, I don't fault Mr. Cowell for doing his job. I get it. In fact, I participated in it. But his criticism was just the beginning of what I experienced because of my audition. Some media critics accused me of perpetuating an Asian stereotype.

They suggested my notoriety would set back legitimate Asian performers in the entertainment industry. That bothers me more than anything Mr. Cowell said to people who auditioned.

Think about what those critics are suggesting when they urge me to step aside for other Asians. Aren't they saying that because other people might stereotype me, that is my problem rather than their problem? And that because I look or talk a certain way, I should go away and hide somewhere so that other, more TV-friendly Asian types should be showcased in the spotlight? I'm reticent to throw around labels, but that strikes me as a soft but insidious form of racism.

I saw and understood how most Asians tended to get mostly negative acting roles, like geeks or prostitutes. However, I haven't and won't apologize for my audition or my subsequent fame. If others want to claim I represent a negative stereotype, they can explain what they mean and try to justify it. Like each of my critics, and for that matter every individual in this world, I am a unique person. Don't I deserve to have dreams like anyone else, and shouldn't I be encouraged to pursue them? Or at the very least, not criticized for doing so because of what I represent racially to some people?

I think we gradually came to accept mean-spiritedness as business as usual. Without delving into politics, we can at least agree that there are accepted norms that have been so shattered by the current Trump administration that we've come to accept them as normal—Twitter rants, political rallies, attacks on the press, the proliferation of lies, things that would never have been tolerated before. The point is, social norms begin to change when they're repeatedly undermined.

This social climate we're in is virtually inhospitable when it comes to courtesy, compassion, and respectfulness. And if *American Idol* played a role in presaging this, in the internet it has found its culmination. And where TV gave us bullies, this new medium has given us trolls.

Don't get me wrong—I'm not a technophobe advocating an off-the-grid lifestyle. TV is here to stay and so is the internet. With that in mind, it is incumbent on those of us who still care to make these communication channels the center for sharing authentic insights and news that actually matter. We must never get to a point in which we just accept that it must be this way.

TURNING YOUR DREAMS INTO REALITY

My vision has changed and evolved over time. When I originally auditioned for *American Idol* in 2004, I wanted to become an entertainer. When I did my first interview with Ryan Seacrest, I determined that there was only a very small chance that the opportunity would do anything for me. But it did. Everything happened in the most surprising and unexpected ways, and I merely allowed myself to embrace the path.

A dream that I dared not even speak aloud had come true.

When a dream is realized, it inspires the dreamer to aim higher and keep reaching. In June 2018, another dream came true: I performed onstage with Ricky Martin!

How? A friend of mine told me that she heard Martin talking about wanting to perform with me on one of the local radio stations in LA. She said I should call the DJ from that radio station. So, I did and it was true. They put me in touch with Ricky Martin's manager, and the next thing I knew, they brought me out to a sold-out crowd at the Monte Carlo where I performed "She Bangs" alongside my college idol, Ricky Martin. It doesn't get any more surreal than that.

When you fulfill one dream, consider it time to get started on another. After I discovered my love of poker, I began fantasizing about playing at the highest level of the game: *The World Series of Poker Main Event.* To give you an idea of how pie in the sky that is, the entry fee alone is a hefty $10,000! That's a big dream. Nevertheless, I dreamt.

I wanted to have the experience but, as you might well imagine, I didn't want to pony up the money to sit at the table. Poker professionals and fans came to my aid, financially assisting me with about 80 percent of my fee. Bottom line: it cost me just $2,000 to achieve that dream.

And now, it's time to dream again. I'm not satisfied with my day job. I believe I have more to offer and I know what I want: To inspire others to follow their dreams, which means helping them dissolve their fears. I wanted to become an international keynote speaker and I was able to achieve that dream, too! I started speaking locally back in 2017, and by 2018, I had the opportunity to inspire people in many different states in America, as well as in Canada and in Singapore. I want to continue to inspire more people to make better choices so they can live their best life, the life they deserve.

That's my dream. What's yours? Are you ready to make the choices necessary to achieve it? Are you ready to become a champion in people's hearts? If you are, the world will be a better place. If you are, then put down this book and start right now. I wish you every success in your noble endeavor to better this world. The world needs you!

ACKNOWLEDGEMENTS

Writing a book is harder than I thought and more rewarding than I could ever imagine. None of this would have been possible without Book Launchers—Julie Broad and her team. They helped me overcome my struggles as a first-time author.

I am eternally grateful to three of my very best friends: Frances Vay and Anna Yang from New York Life, and Amy Lee from HSBC Bank. With their unique backgrounds and experience, they have offered me new perspectives with which to look at my life's challenges. They have helped me celebrate my successes and supported me during times when I felt hopeless.

A special thanks to all of the mentors I have met through Toastmasters International: Carl Walsh, Emi Fukuoka, Mayra Puchalski, Marguerite Piazza Bonnett, and one of the former World Champions of Public Speaking, Craig Valentine.

To Carol Cox from *Speaking Your Brand* for helping me create my new signature talk and for providing the framework for this entire book as well as incredible insights about effective communication.

Writing a book about the story of your life in order to inspire other people to make choices that will help them achieve their dreams is a surreal process. I'm forever indebted to Julie Broad, Scott Bridges, Kelly Ragan, Cathy Reed, and Jacqueline Kyle for their editorial help, keen insights, and ongoing support in bringing my stories to life. It is because of their efforts and encouragement that I have a legacy to pass on to my family and friends.

To my mom and dad, who have helped me balance my relentless optimism with much needed reality checks. They have helped me turn my dreams into goals and my goals into accomplishments.

Finally, to all those who have been a part of my getting there: My coworker friends, Emily Liu and Jane Maynard; my professional poker player friends, Bart Hanson, Ki Lee, Maria Ho, Brian Rast, and Alec Torelli; real estate investor and entrepreneur Leslie Quinsay; mindset mentor Jacqui Letran; and professional speaker Darren Tay.

Made in the USA
Monee, IL
20 December 2022

22854680R00069